# RAIN FOR CHRISTMAS

Written by
## Richard Tulloch

Illustrated by
## Wayne Harris

CAMBRIDGE UNIVERSITY PRESS
Cambridge
New York  Port Chester  Melbourne  Sydney

Not so very long ago on a farm in the outback in the middle of Australia, someone was writing an Important Letter.

To Santa Claus,
c/o The North Pole,
Arctic Ocean,
Northern Hemisphere.

Dear Santa,

For my Christmas presents this year, please could I have a bike and a dolls' house and a new bridle for my pony and some crayons and a pirate hat and a sword and a bottle of pretend blood and a doctor set. And most of all, Santa, I want a boat. Just a little boat that I can sail in the rock pool in our creek.

Love from,
Your friend,
Sally.

P.S. I hope you don't think I'm being greedy, Santa, but you remember last year I asked for a pet carpet snake and you gave me a dumb goldfish instead so I think I ought to get some of my wishes granted this time.
Especially the boat, please.

But Sally knew she wouldn't be able to sail a boat
in the rock pool that year.

That Christmas was bang smack in the middle of
the driest, hottest summer anyone could
remember.

Every blade of grass that poked its head up through the dusty red soil was quickly shrivelled by the burning sun.

The creek had no water in it at all and the rock pool was nothing but a patch of sticky mud.

And when Sally went outside she found a kangaroo, an emu and a cockatoo which had crept out of the bush to beg for a drink from the rain tank.

The water in the rain tank was supposed to be for Sally's family for drinking and washing and brushing their teeth. But during the drought Sally had been taking extra small baths (she didn't like washing much anyway), so she thought it would be all right to give the water she saved to her thirsty animal friends.

She gave them as much water as she dared but she saw that it had turned a dirty brown colour. There was only enough left for a few more days.

If the animals didn't get fresh water soon, Sally knew that they would die.

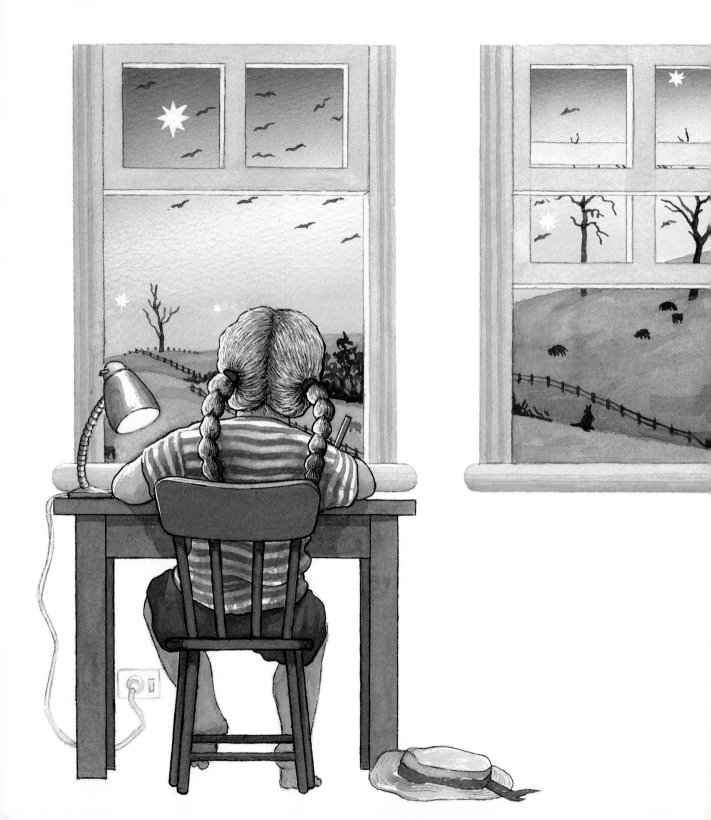

Sally liked to get lots of presents from Santa, but she knew that this year there was something else she had to ask for. So she tore up her Important Letter and wrote a Very Important Letter instead...

Dear Santa,

I don't want any presents this year, but please, please, please could you make it rain on Christmas Day?

Your friend,
Sally.

And quickly, before she could change her mind, she put it in an envelope and posted it to Santa.

Some people say the coldest place in the world is Antarctica and some say it's the top of Mount Everest in a blizzard. Some say that down in the deep dark depths of the ocean where the sun's rays can't reach it's cold enough to freeze a jellyfish. No-one lives at any of these places, so it doesn't really matter what the weather's like there.

But as everyone knows, Santa lives at the North Pole and stuffing the last presents into the bag on his sleigh in the gently falling snow he was finding it quite cold enough thank you very much.

His reindeer, even though they were used to this sort of weather, were grumbling as usual. Reindeer are the world's worst whingers and have as much patience as children queueing up for ice-creams.

"My feet are freezing," said one.
"I think my antlers are growing icicles," shivered another.
"G-g-g-get a move on, S-s-s-santa," said a third, his teeth chattering in the cold, "A t-t-tortoise with rheumatism could load a sleigh f-f-f-faster than that."

"Don't worry, Reindeer," said Santa, "We're ready to take off right now."

But just as the sleigh started moving Santa spotted
the soggy corner of a Very Important Letter
sticking out of the snow.
"What's this? Late mail? Ho, ho, just in time.
I certainly don't want to miss anybody out."
He opened the letter and tried to read the damp,
smudgy writing.

Dear Santa,

I don't want any presents this year,
but please, please, please
could you make it rain
on Christmas Day?

Your friend,
Sally.

"Make it rain on Christmas Day?" said Santa,
"Good heavens, however can I do that?"
He took off his hat to scratch his head, then
quickly put it back on when an icy snowflake
landed on his bald patch. And then he quickly
took it off again because inside his warm hat the
snowflake had melted, sending a little stream of
cold water trickling down the back of his neck.
Then Santa had the most brilliant idea he'd ever
had in all his long life.
"Eureka! I've got it! We can take a giant
snowball to Australia!"

It's a long way from the North Pole to Australia
and by the time they got there the reindeer
were exhausted.

"Can't we stop for a drink?" said one.
"Or a little lie down?" said another.
"Or a long lie down?" said a third.

"No time for that, lads!"
yelled Santa, "We have to
get over the mountain before the
snowball melts!"

"All very well for him to say,"
puffed the reindeer, "That snowball weighs
more than Santa and all the toys put together!"

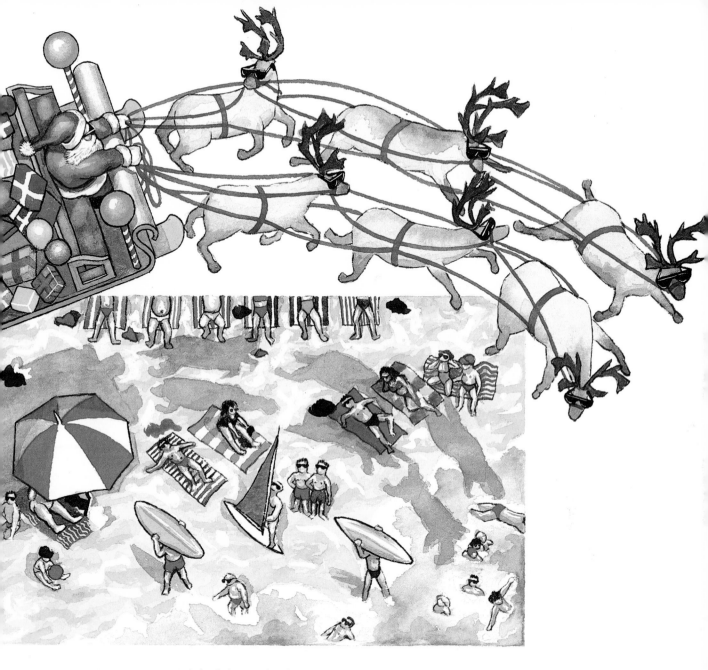

And although they pulled with all their strength
the sleigh sank lower and lower, and by the time
they reached the mountains there was no escape.
They were going to...

... C R

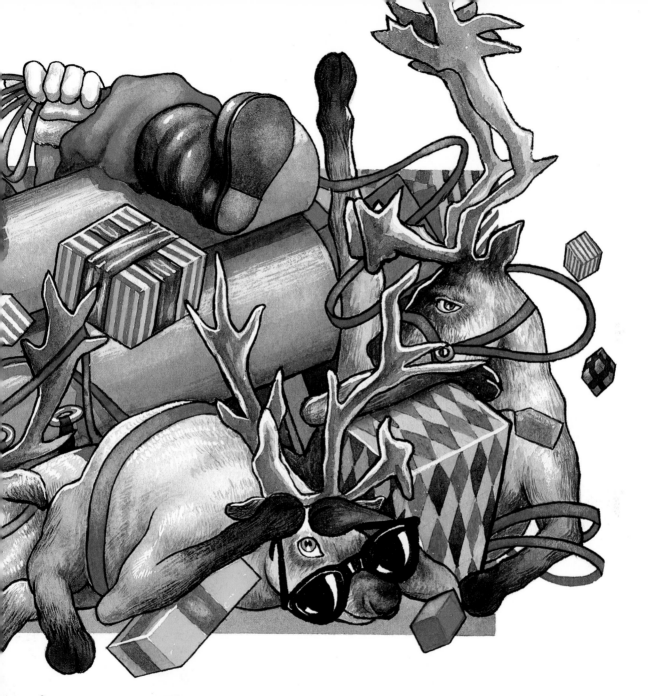

A S H!!

Santa picked himself up and looked around him.

The snowball had rolled away into the undergrowth. His bag had burst open and presents were scattered all through the bush. And beside the upturned sleigh lay his reindeer, so tired that they didn't even have the energy to grumble.

"Don't worry about us, Santa, we're not really hurt," said one.
"We just need a little rest," said another.
"A long rest, actually," added a third.

"Blistering blizzards!" moaned Santa, "Whatever are we going to do? Even if I could find all those presents again I can't deliver them with no-one to pull the sleigh! And how am I going to get that snowball to Sally's place? Freeze my whiskers, what a terrible mess!!!"

For a moment everything was quiet. Then from between the trees came a rustling and a bustling and bright eyes sparkled in the darkness.

Suddenly the bush was alive with animals. Never before had Santa had so many helpers!

Sally woke with a start. A kangaroo was tapping at her window. Which wouldn't have been so surprising, except that her room was on the second floor of the house.

She rubbed her eyes and looked again. Either it was an extremely tall kangaroo or else... There was no mistaking it. The kangaroo was flying! It was one of six, bobbing gently up and down in the air, harnessed to a sleigh crowded with animals and piled high with Christmas presents. And there in the middle of it all was a face she had never seen before, but which she knew as well as she knew her own.

"Sally," beamed Santa, "I really am delighted to meet you. You know, every year I get millions of letters from children all around the world, all asking for presents. So it's a nice change when someone says they don't want any presents and instead asks for something for someone else.

"So how would you like a special treat? How would you like to come for a ride with me? I really need all the helpers I can get tonight. Come on, Sally, what do you say?"

"I say, 'Yes!'" said Sally.

And as they were flying along,
Sally was able to ask Santa
all the questions she'd always wondered
about. Like "How do you fit down the
chimneys?" and "What if there's a fire
in the fireplace?" and "Does your sleigh
ever slide off when it lands on a pointy
roof?" and "Don't you ever get airsick?"

And sometimes Santa answered
"Well..." and sometimes he answered
"Hmmm?" and sometimes he just said
"My, my, Sally, you ask some pretty
tricky questions, don't you?"

MERRY CHRISTMAS

But he did tell her some of his special
secrets and made her promise not to
tell anyone else. Sally did promise
and she crossed her heart so of course
that means she didn't tell me
the secrets and I can't tell you. Sorry.

Then when they'd finished delivering all the presents, the sleigh swooped down into the bush and to Sally's amazement came to a gentle stop beside an enormous snowball.

"Whatever is that doing here, Santa?" she asked.

Santa chuckled as he hitched the snowball up behind the sleigh. "Aha, Sally, that's my most fantabulous secret of all. We're going to make some real magic tonight! Gee-up!"

And the kangaroos pulled the sleigh, with Sally and Santa and the snowball, high into the sky above Sally's farm.

Higher and higher they climbed, right up
to where the stars twinkled all around
them. Three times round the moon they flew, faster and
faster until the snowball burst into a million sparkling pieces,
sending tiny fragments of glittering ice tumbling slowly down
towards the earth.

"I knew it would work!" laughed Santa, "Fantabulous!"

On Christmas morning, Sally woke up in bed...to a noise she hadn't heard for a long, long time.

"Drip, drip, plink, plink, kerplatter..."

It was raining! Not just a passing sun shower, but heavy sheets of rain, lashing across the yard.

Little rivers were pouring off the roof and gushing into the rain tank, while over in the bush kangaroos and emus and wombats and wallabies were lapping water from the puddles that were forming in every gully.

And at the foot of Sally's bed she found a little boat, just the right size for sailing in the rock pool in the creek.

Sally ran to the window and looked up into the sky. "Thank you, Santa!" she breathed, "This is the most fantabulous Christmas present I've ever had in all my life!"

# For Guy and Nathaniel

The right of the
University of Cambridge
to print and sell
all manner of books
was granted by
Henry VIII in 1534.
The University has printed
and published continuously
since 1584.

Published by the Press Syndicate of the University of Cambridge

The Pitt Building, Trumpington Street, Cambridge CB2 1RP, UK
32 East 57th Street, New York, NY 1002, USA
10 Stamford Road, Oakleigh, Melbourne, 3166, Australia

© Cambridge University Press, 1989

First published in 1989

Printed in Hong Kong by Colorcraft Limited

*National Library of Australia cataloguing in publication data*

Tulloch, Richard.
    Rain for Christmas.
    ISBN 0 521 37085 X.
    I. Harris, Wayne. II. Title.
A 823'.3

*British Library cataloguing in publication data*

Tulloch, Richard.
    Rain for Christmas.
    I. Title. II. Harris, Wayne.
    823 (J)
    ISBN 0 521 37085 X.

*Library of Congress cataloguing in publication data*

Tulloch, Richard
    Rain for Christmas.
    Summary: While writing her annual letter to Santa Claus
    during the "driest, hottest summer anyone could remember," a
    young Australian girl decides to ask for rain rather than
    presents and has her request granted in an unusual way.
    [1. Santa Claus – Fiction. 2. Rain and rainfall – Fiction.
    3. Christmas – Fiction. 4. Australia – Fiction.]
    I. Harris, Wayne, ill. II. Title.
    P27.T82315Rai 1989   [E] 89-7159
    ISBN 0 521 37085 X.